# The MEDIA

# Television and Video

MARSHALL CAVENDISH
New York London Toronto Sydney

**Reference Edition Published 1989**

Published by Marshall Cavendish Corporation
147 West Merrick Road
Freeport, Long Island
N.Y. 11520

Editor: Susannah Foreman
Designer: David Armitage

Reference edition produced by DPM Services Limited

Consultant Editor: Maggi McCormick
Art Editor: Graham Beehag

Printed in Italy by G. Canale C.S.p.A., Turin
Bound in Italy by L.E.G.O. S.p.A., Vicenza


**Library of Congress Cataloging-in-Publication Data**

Alvarado, Manuel.
    Television and video / Manuel Alvarado
        p. cm. – (The Media)
    Bibliography: p.
    Includes index
    Summary: Explores the content and method of
presentation of television and video as a media and the effect
these have on our lives.
    ISBN 0-86307-974-1
    ISBN 0-86307-973-3 (Set)
    1. Television broadcasting – Juvenile literature. 2. Video
recordings – Juvenile literature. [1. Television broadcasting,
2. Video recordings.] I. Title. II. Series. Media (New York,
N.Y.)
PN1992.57.A49 1989
384.55'4–dc 19                                88-29535
                                                  CIP
                                                  AC

# Contents

# 1 | History and Development

## ● THE BEGINNINGS

In 1936, the first regular television broadcast in the U.S. was made by Radio Corporation of America to 150 homes in New York. Later the same year, the British Broadcasting Corporation (BBC), began regular broadcasts from London, transmitted twice a day. Simultaneously, but not on a regular basis, Germany was also experimenting with television broadcasting, as were a number of other countries.

In fact, the idea of being able to transmit images and sounds simultaneously over the airwaves had been around for a long time. As early as 1875, there had been many technological inventions that were eventually to be used in the development of television, but

*All modern television broadcasting has its origins in the experiments and developments that took place in Europe and the U.S. in the 1920s and 30s.*

Emitron 405-line electronic scanning system. The BBC could not decide which system was better and therefore compromised by transmitting the two systems, using each on alternate weeks. If you owned only one type of television set, you could watch only one week in every two! However, the Emitron was soon to prove itself as the superior system, and by the time that World War II began, the BBC had made a wide range of programs, including 326 plays.

On the day Britain declared war with Germany — September 1, 1939 — television was closed down. The last item was a Mickey Mouse cartoon, and, imitating the accent of the Swedish actress Greta Garbo, his last words were, "Ah tink ah go home." The screen went blank, and there was no closing announcement. Television was closed down for fear that German planes might use the transmission signals as homing devices for bombing runs on London.

it is a Scottish engineer — John Logie Baird — who is generally credited with the first practical demonstration of television. Using a mechanical scanning system, Baird experimented in his workshop on the top floor of one of London's large department stores. He gave his first successful demonstration of television by mechanically scanning a screen made up of 25 lines in 1926.

Baird spent the next ten years experimenting with and improving his system, but enthusiasts who bought or built the early receivers (which cost as much as a small car) had to telephone him after transmission to check on what they had been watching!

By the time the BBC agreed to undertake regular daily transmissions, however, Baird's 240-line mechanical scanning system had a competitor. In 1932, EMI had introduced their

*Right* The last program to be broadcast by the BBC on the day war was declared in 1939 was a Mickey Mouse cartoon.

# ● DEVELOPMENTS

Television experiments were conducted throughout the same period in the United States. Herbert Hoover appeared as a presidential candidate in an experimental AT&T television broadcast in 1927. There were many important engineers working in the field at the time including Vladimir Zworykin and Edwin H. Armstrong, but it is generally considered that the young inventor Philo T. Farnsworth probably made the greatest breakthrough. He recognized from the beginning how inadequate a mechanical scanning system was with its clumsy rotating discs. He finally managed to patent his electronic device in 1930, despite attempts by the Radio Corporation of America (RCA) to stop him, as they, too, were working in the field

*Below* A modern Columbia Broadcasting System (CBS) television cameraman. CBS began television broadcasting in the 1930s.

*Above* David Sarnoff, head of CBS in the 1930s, played an important role in the development of American television.

of television technology. By 1932, the National Broadcasting Company (NBC) had installed a television studio in the Empire State Building. In 1933, David Sarnoff, head of the Columbia Broadcasting System (CBS) and the most important business figure in the history of the early development of American television, moved to Radio City, New York, where he based his television operations.

Television technology developed rapidly throughout the 1930s, but it was not until April 30, 1939, (ironically the year television was closed down in Britain), that television was formally opened by Franklin D. Roosevelt, who became the first American president to appear on the screen. An early RCA set cost between $200 and $600.

During the first year of operation, expansion was rapid. By May, 1940, there were 23 stations broadcasting television in the U.S., but problems about commercial advertising led television to revert to "experimental" status for a year. The following year (1941), television finally accepted advertising but even then

*A man watching a tiny early American television screen during the 1930s.*

schedules were soon reduced from 15 to 4 hours a week, and only six stations serving 10,000 sets remained in business.

Broadcasting in the U.S. was stopped when the nation entered World War II, and it was not until the middle of 1946 that television began to get underway seriously in both Britain and the U.S. By this time, the technology had improved considerably, and as a direct result of the development of radar during the war, there was now a growing number of fully trained personnel, who had previously used their skills to operate radar equipment. While Britain had opted for a national non-commercial broadcasting system from the beginning, the situation in the U.S. was more uneven. New York and Los Angeles had seven fully operational stations by 1952, but some major cities had no television at all.

Nevertheless, for 30 years, television was little more than an enthusiasts' hobby. However, in June, 1946, the *Washington Post* alerted its readers to the possibilities of the future when it reported the televising of the Joe Louis — Billy Conn boxing match, saying "Television looks good for a 1,000 year run."

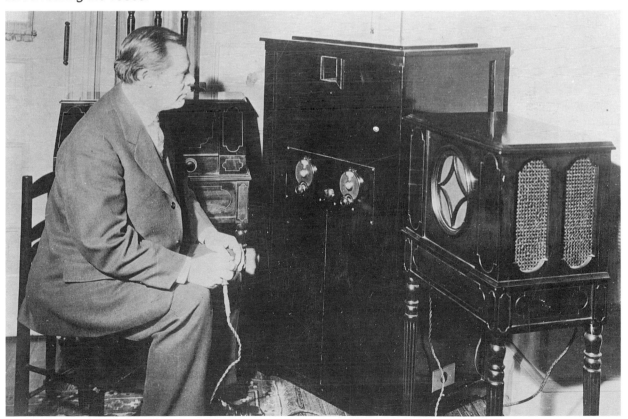

# ● FURTHER TECHNICAL DEVELOPMENTS

Since the pioneering days, there have been numerous technical developments. From 1941, American innovators experimented with the use of color, and a regular nationwide service was introduced by CBS on June 25, 1951. In Britain, color was introduced as late as 1969, by which time the original 405-line screen had been replaced with the higher definition 625 system (American television still has 525 lines). Britain had also taken its time to adopt color broadcasting because there were three different color systems — the USA's NTSC, France's SECAM, and West Germany's PAL.

There have also been experiments with 3D images, stereophonic sound, and, most recently, High Definition Television (HDTV). Many years ago, France had experimented with an 819-line system, and the Sony Corporation of Japan is currently trying to establish its 1125-line, wide screen, hi-fi sound system. For screens as big as a medium-size movie theater, the system gives a picture as high in quality as that of the always superior 35mm film image. The problem with this new system is that its introduction would involve replacing literally every piece of television production, transmission, and reception equipment in the world. Europe has been fighting back with the development of the British designed C-MAC and D2-MAC systems, which claim to provide High Definition Television without having to change current equipment.

However, the development of video technology has transformed the use of television far more than most pioneers in the industry could ever have conceived.

# ● VIDEO

John Baird experimented with video discs in 1928, but it was an American company, Ampex, that first demonstrated and marketed videotape equipment in 1956. Ampex has always produced equipment intended for broadcast television, and their machines transformed television production practices. But it was Sony's domestic equipment that not only transformed, but actually revolutionized television use. As far back as 1948, when the company was developing cassette tape recorders, Sony had been investigating the possibility of recording images on magnetic tape — a project that they took on in earnest in 1953.

It was another 16 years before the first Sony domestic systems (black and white, reel to reel) appeared and a further five before the first color cassette machines were introduced by the Dutch company Philips. Four more years of research and development resulted in the appearance of the first reliable domestic machines in 1978, using the two formats that currently dominate the field — VHS (Video Home System) and Betamax.

The instant popularity of video staggered the media world. By comparison, television had grown slowly. In 1982, there were 13 million

video recorders around the world, but by 1986, this figure had grown to over 120 million, half of which were sold in the previous two years. In Britain, for example, one home in two possesses a video recorder.

*Below* A modern Sony High Definition television receiver (**left**) and (**right**) a High Definition professional video recorder.

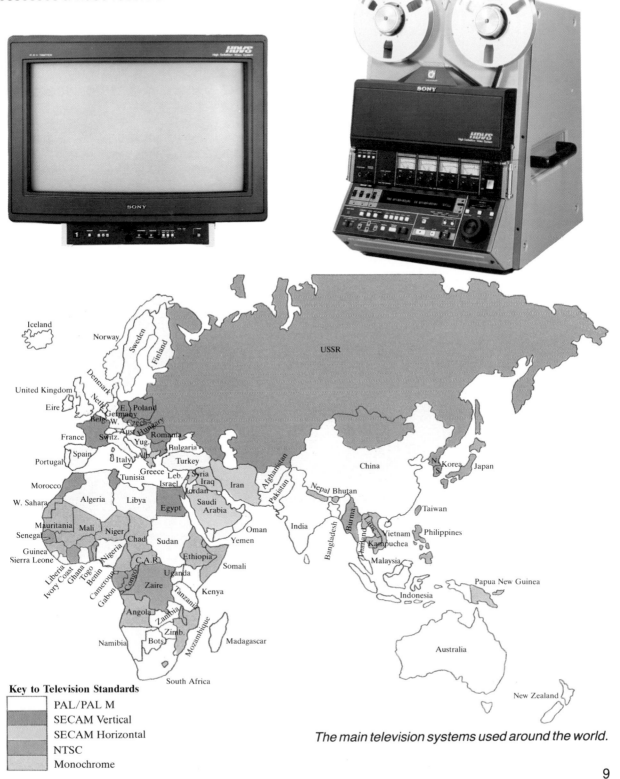

**Key to Television Standards**

PAL/PAL M
SECAM Vertical
SECAM Horizontal
NTSC
Monochrome

*The main television systems used around the world.*

# 2 Broadcasting Institutions

We tend to accept the television programs we watch without thinking too much about who was responsible for them, who made them, and how they were made. However, once we begin to watch programs from other countries, we immediately begin to see differences.

These differences are due partly to the fact that individual producers view the world in different ways and that broadcasting varies in its organization in different places. Television institutions are structured, organized, financed, and regulated in a variety of ways, and these differences will be reflected in the sort of programs that are made. Therefore, in order to understand television better, we need to know something about the systems of different countries.

*An NBC television camera covering a football game for a live network transmission.*

# ● THE UNITED STATES

*30 Rockefeller Plaza, New York City, is the home of NBC, one of the world's largest commercial television companies.*

There are more television sets (145 million) in the U.S. than in any other country in the world, and the average American watches more than seven hours of television a day. The three American TV networks, ABC (American Broadcasting Company) NBC, and CBS, are also the world's three largest commercial television companies. However, with the exception of news and sports programs, these companies make very few of their own programs. Instead, they buy programs primarily from independent producers, many of them based in Hollywood.

These three companies have dominated American television for four decades, but they have been restricted from further expansion by the national regulatory body, the Federal Communications Commission (FCC). This body was created out of the old Federal Radio Commission in 1934 and is responsible for regulating broadcasting in the U.S. For example, until 1985, a company could own no more than 7 (now 12) television stations. As a result, ABC, NBC, and CBS have each created large systems of networks affiliates, which are companies around the country that have special distribution and broadcasting agreements.

All the major dramas, such as *Dallas, Dynasty, Miami Vice, LA Law, The A-Team,* and *The Cosby Show* were screened for the first time by the networks. These programs attract huge audiences, so the companies are able to charge the highest rates for advertising time during these programs. Competition within American commercial television is about delivering the highest number of viewers to the advertisers. The fact that programs are popular is simply a means to an end.

This is the wealthiest layer of American television. On the second layer are the independent companies, which have grown enormously in recent years. There are approximately 300 companies covering the 67 major cities in the U.S. (before 1980, only the top 30 were covered), with cities such as New York supporting a number of such stations. These stations produce their own news, and occasionally talk shows, but most of their schedules are made up of sydicated repeats of network hits. In response to the domination of the networks over the American system, these companies have devised one strategy known as "stripping," where they play the same series in the same slot five or six nights a week. Clearly, this involves broadcasting series with many episodes if it is going to feature regularly in the schedule. Long-running programs, like *M.A.S.H.* with its 251 episodes, are ideal for syndicating in this way. Other shows, all hits in their heyday and many of which have strong cult followings, are scheduled in weekly slots in a bid to attract viewers away from the networks.

The third major sector of American television is the national Public Broadcasting System (PBS), which is financed partly by the federal government, partly by local donations and subscriptions, and partly by commercial sponsorship, most notably from the oil companies. The system, which has no commercials, has struggled financially during the last twenty years. Regular requests appear on the screen asking for donations, and sponsorship "statements" precede and follow sponsored programs. Because PBS cannot afford to fill its schedule entirely with original "quality" programs, it has to buy a fair proportion of programs from television companies overseas. A great many of these purchases come from Britain, which has led to the joke that PBS stands for Primarily British Series!

*M.A.S.H., with its 251 episodes, is ideal for "stripping:" showing the same series at the same time for 5 or 6 nights a week.*

# ● BRITAIN

The organization of television in Great Britain is quite different. In line with all the other European countries, British television has always been organized on the principles of public service broadcasting. Both the BBC and the commercial television companies are required to "inform, educate, and entertain" the audience and thereby to provide a balanced diet of programs — drama, light entertainment, news, documentaries, current affairs, sports, and religion. Broadcasting in Europe is not seen as a commercial enterprise undertaken purely for profit, as it generally is in the U.S., but is seen instead as a public utility — something that everybody can switch on, like turning on a faucet or an electric light.

The operation of this principle is best

*BBC Television Center, Shepherd's Bush, West London. This is the BBC's main television studio complex.*

explained by outlining the structure of British broadcasting. Basically, it consists of two complementary systems. The first is the BBC, which is a corporation originally founded as a commercial company in 1922, but established as a public corporation by Royal Charter in 1926. It is almost wholly funded by a licence fee payment (currently £58) which is paid annually by everybody who owns or rents a TV set. Out of this money, the BBC is required to run two television channels, four national radio stations, and approximately 50 local radio stations. With a staff of approximately 30,000 and an annual income of £933 million, it is by far the world's single largest broadcasting organization.

The second system is the Independent Television system (ITV), which was established by Act of Parliament in 1954. Since it began operations in 1955, ITV has been financed almost totally by advertising.

Whereas the BBC is a national system based in London, ITV is regionally organized with 15 companies covering 14 regions (London is covered by two companies, one for weekdays and one for weekends) all governed by the Independent Broadcasting Authority (IBA). Unlike the American system, the commercial stations do not compete for audiences, and therefore for advertising revenue, either with each other *or* with the BBC. Competition between the stations is primarily focused upon the quality and success of programs.

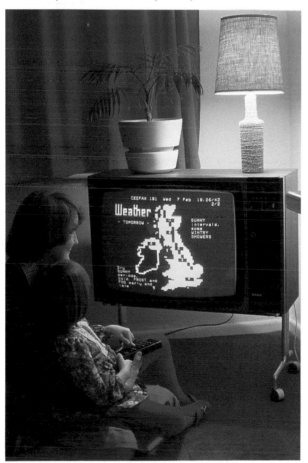

*The BBC's teletext system, Ceefax, offers hundreds of pages of information on news, sports, the weather, financial markets, and many other subjects, at the touch of a button.*

Both systems are governed by Boards of Governors, who are appointed by the government to be responsible for running the BBC and the IBA, but who are also supposed to protect the systems from direct governmental interference. Broadcasting therefore appears to be independent of the government of the day, although in practice there are many examples of governments trying to influence contentious programs and broadcasting decisions.

Since 1982, two new national commercial broadcasting organizations have been established — TV-AM, which is responsible for commercial breakfast-time TV, and Channel 4, the second ITV channel, which is different enough to constitute a third strand in television broadcasting in Britain.

Providing the first national commercial TV service (with the exception of Wales which has its own, largely Welsh language, version, S4C) Channel 4 operates very like a book publishing house. The company produces hardly any programs itself. Instead, it commissions programs either from the existing ITV companies or, more significantly, from small independent companies. The creation of this

**Above** *Anthony Higgins in Peter Greenaway's* The Draughtsman's Contract, *a film financed by Channel 4 and the British Film Institute.*

one company has transformed the nature of British television production. It has also greatly improved the work possibilities for independent program makers.

**Below** *ITV's early morning television company, TV AM, is housed in a futuristic complex near Camden Lock in North London.*

# ● WESTERN EUROPE

All the Western European countries run their broadcasting systems along public service lines, with a licence fee being charged as in Britain. Two of them still do not allow any commercial television at all, and Iceland broadcasts only six nights a week, partly in order to encourage people to do things other than watch television.

The system in each country is slightly different. The Dutch system of broadcasting claims to have the most democratically accountable system in the world. The system is arranged to give broadcasting time to organizations representing the whole range of Dutch religious and political groups according to the size of their membership. An organization with a great many members is given a large amount of broadcasting time, while one with a relatively small membership will be allowed only a few hours. These allocations change if membership size changes. Broadcasting is financed by licence fee, with a small amount of advertising presented (as is the case in a number of Western European countries) in blocks at certain times of the evening. In the case of Holland, these blocks are five minutes long, occur six times in the evening, and are not allowed on Sundays.

*A scene from Schwarzwaldklinik (Black Forest Clinic), a successful West German soap opera, which has been shown in Britain and the U.S.*

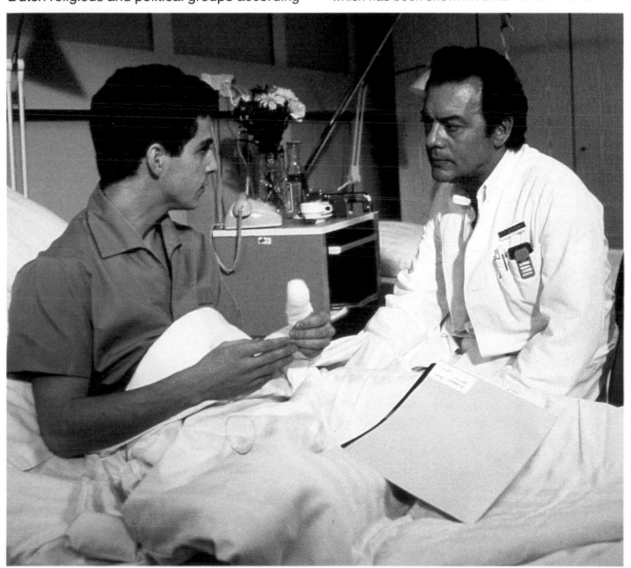

Italy has a different system. Until 1976, television was run by the state broadcast network, RAI (Radiotelevisione Italiana). Then, the Italian Constitutional Court declared, in a very dramatic judgment, that the public service monopoly of broadcasting was unconstitutional except at the national level. This decision, known as deregulating, opened the gate to a proliferation of small regional stations; by the early 1980s, there were approximately 1,500. The result was a weakening of Italian television production, as

*Inside the studio of the Nederlandse Omroep Stichting (NOS-TV) in Hilversum, Holland, with a show in progress.*

these small stations bought cheap foreign imports instead of financing domestic production. Furthermore, as RAI lost its majority audience in this move, it has found it very difficult to maintain its high level of production.

Italy's experience has made the other European countries very wary of allowing deregulation in their own countries.

# ● AUSTRALIA

Australia offers yet another system of broadcasting, which manages to combine both the European and the American models and programs at the same time. Television was not established until 1957, but both the state broadcaster — the Australian Broadcasting Corporation (ABC) — and four commercial companies started transmitting at the same time in the country's two largest cities, Sydney and Melbourne. Since then, broadcasting has greatly expanded, and there are now 86 ABC stations and 50 commercial companies.

Australian television produces a fair number of its own programs (a number of which are seen regularly on daytime television: *Sons and Daughters, A Country Practice, The Sullivans, Neighbours*), and it also imports many programs from both Britain and the U.S. This can lead to interesting situations where

Australians can see both the British and the American version of a situation comedy based on the same idea and characters, such as *Steptoe and Son* and *Sanford and Son*.

A unique experiment in Australian broadcasting was started in 1980, called Channel 0/28 — Multicultural Television. This channel transmits films, drama series, and soap operas from all over the world (in their original languages) and has news programs that use foreign news clips not shown on either the ABC or the commercial channels. It is intended for the sizeable ethnic communities in the two largest cities, but many people watch it in order to gain alternative views of the world's cultures and events.

*Gus Mercurio in* Cash & Co., *one of the first Australian series to be sold successfully around the world in the late 1970s.*

# 3 News and Sport

News is generally considered to be the prestige area of television production. It is the basic element of any serious broadcaster's schedule and, given that most news programs are shot in tiny studios with a minimum of cameras, lights, sets, and presenters, such programs are surprisingly expensive to produce. The reason is, of course, that there are huge back-up services involved in any quality news bulletin.

It is rare these days for a major national news program to run a story without some film footage or even a television reporter speaking from the scene of the action. For a national story, this footage could involve the use of a costly outside broadcast (OB) unit, complete with full camera and technical crew and video recording and editing facilities, together with radio link-ups, or a film crew complete with despatch riders who can get the film back to the studio for processing and editing.

For an international story, footage can be bought from one of the commercial news services or from another television organization via satellite. Eurovision link-ups were originally established to make this possible, and, while they are expensive, they are not as costly as sending out a full camera crew. However, if the story is important enough, a full crew with reporter will be sent out, particularly if the story is going to run for some time (as in the case of the Ethiopian famine).

Back in the studio itself, there is an expensive variety of technical facilities and personnel, available at a moment's notice. There are likely to be researchers on call to locate historical film footage if required, a film library, graphics studios and artists, and a wide range of technicians and technical facilities. There will also be a team of reporters and announcers.

*The main television control room in Independent Television News' headquarters in Central London.*

## ● BRITISH TV NEWS

In Britain, the BBC has always prided itself on its coverage of world events, a tradition dating back to World War II. At that time, the BBC World Service was seen (or rather heard) as the voice of the free world reporting against the radio propaganda being pumped out by Hitler's Germany. The ITV companies also pride themselves on their news service, which is provided by their jointly-owned company ITN (Independent Television News). This news service is produced by a separate company as a guarantee that the commercial demands of advertising do not influence editorial news decisions.

These two organizations produce over 60 hours of news a week, transmitted at regular hours throughout the day and evening. In line with the public service principles of British broadcasting, both these organizations are required, as far as possible, to provide a balanced bulletin showing both sides of a story, as is the case in the United States. However, in Britain, there is an unwritten agreement between the four channels to stagger their news bulletins, so that a viewer can tune in to a news bulletin at various times during prime time, which eliminates the competition for advertising between rival channels.

*Right An Outside Broadcast Unit, which relays and broadcasts live from an important outdoor event.*

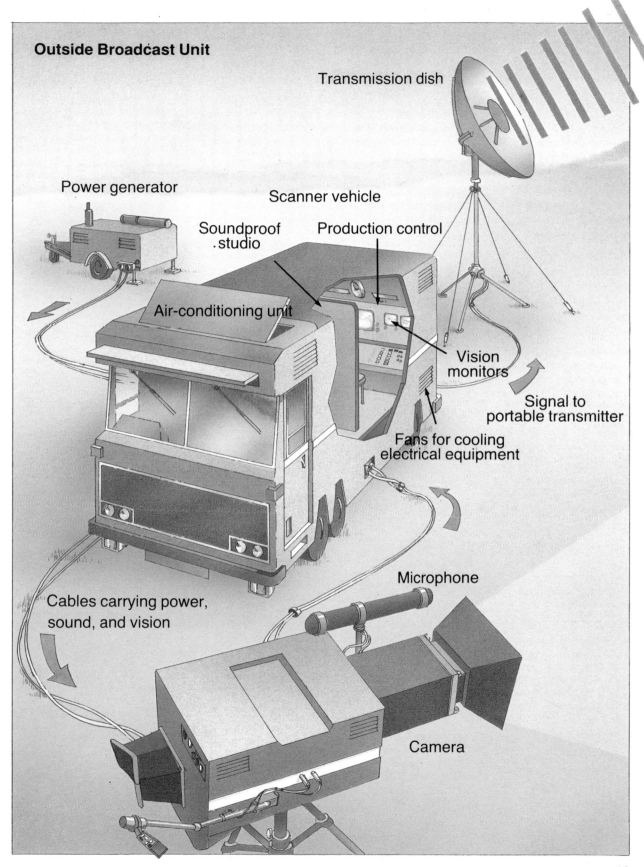

**Outside Broadcast Unit**

Transmission dish

Power generator

Scanner vehicle

Soundproof studio

Production control

Air-conditioning unit

Vision monitors

Signal to portable transmitter

Fans for cooling electrical equipment

Microphone

Cables carrying power, sound, and vision

Camera

19

# ● AMERICAN TV NEWS

In the U.S., the three networks produce their own news programs and spend vast sums on what they consider to be the most important part of their schedules. The main news bulletins of all three compete directly on the 7.00 evening slot, and they therefore use the news to engage in a ratings battle for advertising. Each of them spends in excess of $200 million a year to produce approximately two and a half hours of news a day. In addition to the huge technological resources these companies have at home, a great deal of their money is spent to maintain large permanent overseas news teams based on the major capital cities of the world.

News broadcasting has altered since the arrival of Cable News Network (CNN), headed by the flamboyant Ted Turner. This satellite-fed channel provides a 24-hour news service for the 31 million homes that are hooked to a cable system. Turner, in effect, challenged the three networks, and spent only a quarter of their news expenditure ($50 million) on his non-stop news show.

Turner is a wealthy man and was able to continue despite losing huge sums of money initially. His losses were due partly to the fact that ABC responded to his challenge by launching their own 24-hour news channel, SNC (Satellite News Channel). However, SNC failed. Having successfully weathered that storm, Turner is now selling his channel to European cable systems, and he claims that he will be making a profit by the 1990s.

**Above** Multi-millionaire Ted Turner, ex-racing yachtsman turned media magnate, who owns the world's first 24-hour television news service, Cable News Network (CNN).

**Left** The CBS News outside broadcast booth at the launch of an American space shuttle flight from Cape Kennedy in Florida. CBS has an enormous worldwide news-gathering organization.

TEMPERATURE        30°
HUMIDITY          69%
WINDS          SSE  5
PRESSURE        30.47
AIR QUALITY        19

# ● EUROPEAN TV NEWS

*NBC weatherman Willard Scott. Television weathermen in the U.S. are not expert meteorologists, but are experienced broadcasters.*

How do the news systems of other countries manage? The richer nations such as Britain, West Germany, and France are able to employ correspondents in important "news countries" around the world who phone in stories, which are often broadcast over an image of the city from which they are reporting. They also hire a local film crew or sometimes fly out a crew of their own if the story is considered to be big enough.

In addition, both the eastern and western

European countries exchange news with each other via two systems — "Intervision" and "Eurovision." Through these systems, European countries can exchange news items with each other via satellite and cable links. However, more important in a global sense are the two main television international news agencies — Visnews (which provides approximately 25 percent of Eurovision's news material) and UPITN.

## ● INTERNATIONAL NEWS AGENCIES

Visnews is a predominantly British company owned mainly by the BBC and the international press news service, Reuters. The public service broadcasting organizations of Canada, Australia, and New Zealand also own a small share. UPITN is owned by UPI, the American international press agency and the British commercial news service ITN. Between them, these two large organizations provide a cheap news service worldwide. There are a few other small news agencies, such as CBS, which sell their own stories independently.

The English-language media dominates the world market in news material and sells it just like any other commodity. This makes good business sense for the companies involved, but it also means that much of the material available worldwide gives a rather Anglo-American view of world affairs.

While the richer countries can afford to produce most of their own international news, the poorer countries buy their news material from news services. As a result, a number of news services have been set up to try to offer an alternative version of world events. Two of the best known receive support from UNESCO (the United Nations' Education, Science, and Cultural Organization). They are the agencies serving Africa and the Caribbean — PANA (the Pan-African News Agency) and CANA (the Caribbean News Agency). However, neither of them provides television material.

*Pakistan Television (PTV) is a state-owned company. Its national news service provides three newscasts, one in Urdu, one in Arabic, and one in English.*

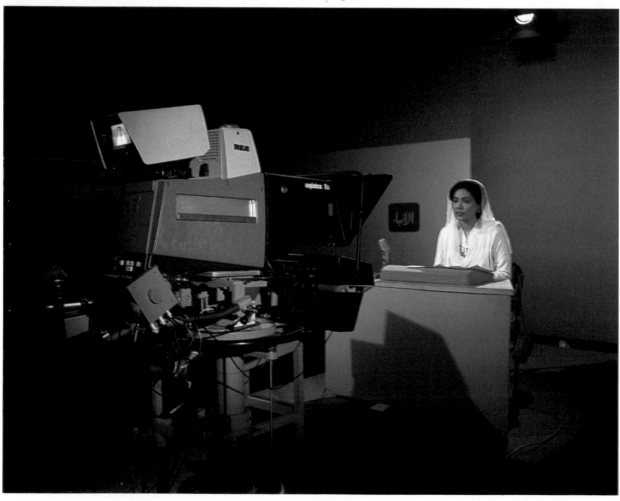

# ● SPORTS NEWS

Sports have become one of the major elements of television broadcasting. Or, to put it another way, television has become one of the most important elements of any national or international sports event. The British media spends £40 million ($70 million) a year covering sports events. A quarter of all the BBC's production is taken up with sports. Events that were once seen as largely national, such as Wimbledon or the FA Cup Final for soccer, are now, thanks to satellites, relayed throughout the world. The potential audience for what were once considered minority interest sports, such as Formula One Grand Prix racing, is now one and a half billion people.

In fact, many sports would have difficulty

*Many sports, such as rugby, now reach a very wide audience, because of live television coverage that can be broadcast around the world.*

surviving on a large scale without television. In 1986, the Wimbledon tennis championships made £6.2 million ($11 million) profit, and received £8.5 million ($15 million) from television. World Cup soccer could not survive without the money paid by the world's media for transmission rights.

However, while television has increasingly helped to finance and support sports events (and has also created a mass audience for what were, until a few years ago, quite marginal games, such as snooker and darts), in the U.S., television has totally transformed sports events.

*Left Football, once the all-American game, is now a big audience draw in many other countries.*

In certain cases, television has actually changed the structure of some sports. "Television time-outs" are co-ordinated in football games by television producers to coincide with commercial breaks, worth doing when the cost of one minute of advertising during the 1987 Super Bowl was $600,000 a minute! The referees are in radio contact with the control room and start and stop play as instructed.

Television has had an effect on many sports around the world. For example, English cricket, which was traditionally a five-day game, now has a popular one-day version that lends itself to television coverage. Tie-breakers have been introduced into some sports for the first time; equipment has been modified so that it shows up better on the screen. Some examples are yellow tennis balls, white cricket balls, and different colored team uniforms, particularly for cricket players who traditionally wore white on both sides. World heavyweight Boxing Championship fights are fought in various cities around the world, sometimes in the middle of the night, so that live coverage can be screened at the most popular viewing time in the U.S.

But the ultimate sporting spectacle for television is the Olympics. Coverage of the Mexican Olympics in 1968 cost $4 million. The rights for the 1988 Winter Olympics at Calgary were sold for a staggering $309 million.

*Television coverage means that cricket can now be seen by audiences around the world.*

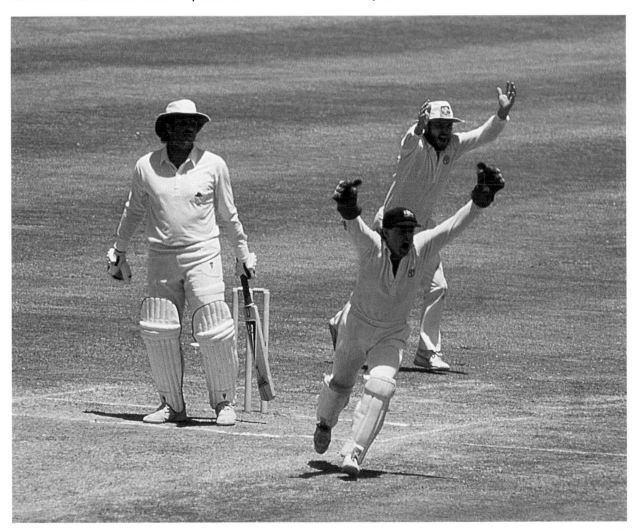

# 4 Television Drama

People are now able to watch sports on television that they would not even have known about in the days before mass media coverage. In a similar way, television has brought drama to a wider audience. As the critic Raymond Williams has observed, people in the television age experience more drama in a week than was previously possible in a lifetime. And if news is the most important area for television companies, it is the drama department that earns the bulk of the international profits.

Drama is the most expensive area of television production. As a rough guide, an hour of British television drama costs about £250,000 ($425,000) while *Dallas* — one of the most expensive programs in the U.S. is

reputed to cost $1 million an episode.

Home-produced television drama has always been extremely popular, but in the 1980s, we have witnessed the phenomenon of the international blockbuster, such as *Dallas* or *Dynasty*. How are they produced and who is involved?

## ● DRAMA PRODUCTION

There are three types of television drama: single plays, series, and serials. Single plays are similar to theatrical plays, but the others are fairly specific to television. Series are programs that feature the same stars and the same locations from week to week, but have a completely different story each episode. Serials, also known as "soap operas" or "soaps," continue the storyline from week to week. Good examples of series are crime fiction programs such as *Miami Vice, Dempsey and Makepeace, Bergerac*, and *Bellamy*. Such programs are shot either on film or on videotape (and occasionally on both). There are various ways of telling on which they are

*Sue Devaney (**left**) and Maureen Lipman in* Exclusive Yarns, *a drama production by TVS — the ITV contractor for the south of England.*

*Programs shot on location usually need only one camera and one camera crew. This camera operator is recording film for Zimbabwean TV.*

recorded. A general rule is that if most of the scenes take place indoors, they are shot on tape, and if most of the action takes place outside, they are shot on film. Why is this distinction important?

Recording on videotape involves the use of a large studio complex with approximately eight sets on the studio floor, at least three cameras, three separate control rooms (one each for light, sound, and vision) and in the region of 100 people working simultaneously on the production. These people will include performers, camera, lighting, and sound crew, electricians, set builders, decorators, and the production team. After the script is written, the team will rehearse the production for ten days. Then they move into a studio and record a one-hour show in two days. The program then enters the post-production stage, when it will be edited and the sound re-mixed. The whole production usually takes between six weeks to

two months.

Programs shot on location on film will usually need only one camera and one camera crew consisting of eight people. A maximum of five minutes of program will be recorded each day; therefore, it will take at least two weeks to record the whole episode. For many reasons, while less people are involved in a film shoot, the costs are usually considerably higher than recording in a studio. However, may program makers prefer to use film because they prefer the "realistic" effect that working in real locations can give to a film.

In the early days of television, the most successful series were Westerns, which had been very popular as movies, so the tradition was carried over into television. Westerns were shot on film *and* were usually made only in the U.S. — Hyde Park in London could not pass for Monument Valley! However, the 1960s saw the emergence of the police series, which was more easily copied in foreign locations. The genre that has maintained its importance and popularity to this day.

# ● COP SHOWS

In the 1950s, the most popular "cop shows" were *Highway Patrol* in the U.S. and *Dixon of Dock Green* in Britain; in the 1960s came *Dragnet* and the British *Z Cars*. The 1970s brought *Kojak* and *The Streets of San Francisco*; Britain responded with *The Sweeney* and *Gangsters*. The 1980s have brought many new variations — *Miami Vice, Moonlighting, LA Law, Hill Street Blues*, and *Cagney and Lacey* from the U.S. and *Minder, Bergerac, The Chinese Detective*, and *The Gentle Touch* from Britain. France, West Germany, Italy, Japan, Brazil, and Australia all have their home-grown equivalents.

Police dramas continue to be popular for several reasons. One is the star status of the performers. Once an actor or actress is

**Above** *Telly Savalas as the lollipop-sucking tough New York detective Kojak, in the American series of the same name.*

established as a star, then viewers will be inclined to return week after week to watch them. Telly Savalas, Jack Webb, Dennis Waterman, and Jill Gascoigne have all become well known through cop shows.

A second factor is the long-established popularity of crime faction. Cop shows always offer a riddle, a mystery that has to be solved. Most episodes try to unravel a problem posed at the beginning. The genre has been popular for at least a hundred years. In the nineteenth century, Sherlock Holmes novels and short stories were widely read; during this century, crime writers such as Agatha Christie and Raymond Chandler have been among the most popular novelists of all. The Hollywood film industry has made hundreds of crime films, and now television continues this tradition.

*Jack Warner as the police sergeant in* Dixon of Dock Green, *the celebrated long-running early BBC television series.*

**Right** *Women cops in action in the popular series* Cagney and Lacey. *British cop shows with women stars include* Juliet Bravo *and* The Gentle Touch.

# ● SERIALS

Serials, which include "soap operas" and mini-series, are "running" dramas in which the viewer has to tune in the next episode to find out "what happens." The term "soap" dates back to the 1930s. It was then that soap powder manufacturers realized that, by sponsoring radio programs about family and domestic affairs during the day, they could reach an audience made up largely of housewives who would, they hoped, buy their products. In the U.S. this term stuck and now applies to daytime television dramas. Prime time programs that occur as serials, such as *Dallas, Dynasty*, and *The Colbys*, are not

thought of as "soaps" in the U.S. The situation is different in Europe and the rest of the world. In Britain, for example, there are different types of program that are classified as soaps.

First there are home-produced soaps, of which there are currently four, that are broadcast early in the evening. Some have topped the ratings for many years. They are supposed to represent the lives of ordinary "working class" or "lower middle class" people living in different regions of Britain. Two are set in the Northwest, one in the Northeast, one in the Midlands, and one in the East End of

*The cost of an eposode of* Dallas *is reputed to be in the region of $1 million. It is financially the most successful program in the world.*

London (a traditionally working class area).

*Dallas* and the other popular American programs shown in Britain are also called soaps, although they, of course, represent a different social class — they offer a picture of lavish wealth. They are shown in prime time on British television, and although they sometimes reach the top of the ratings, they are never as consistently successful as the home-produced soaps. The same is true across the world. *Dallas* is historically the most financially successful program worldwide, but it rarely beats a nation's home-produced programs for consistent popularity.

*Tycoon Jason Colby (Charlton Heston) finally marries Francesca, his sister-in-law, (Katherine Ross) in the popular American series,* The Colbys.

Australian television is also a prolific producer of soap operas, such as *A Country Practice, The Sullivans, Neighbours*, and *Sons and Daughters*. They are syndicated in many foreign markets, and in many places they provide a source of cheap drama for low-audience daytime viewing. They are different from both American and British soap operas in that they represent an essentially middle class society.

# ● WORLD RESPONSES

As already stated, although American series have gained domination of the world's markets, home-produced serials are always more popular with a domestic audience. In Britain, *Coronation Street, Brookside*, and *EastEnders* consistently top the ratings with the widest audiences. These programs are distinctly, parochially, British and non-glamorous, so they are unlikely ever to become major international successes, although they do occasionally appear on screens in other countries.

However, a number of countries have decided to try to compete with the U.S. in this field. The British have not, partly because they are already the world's second largest exporter of television programs, and because the nearest British equivalents, such as the sea-faring drama *Howard's Way*, have had mixed results on the international market. The two countries that have tried hardest in this field are West Germany with *Schwarzwaldklinik* (Black Forest Clinic) and France with *Chateauvallon*. The West German program, which features complex plots and glamorous characters, is set in a wealthy and exclusive health clinic in Germany's Black Forest. *Chateauvallon* is set in the beautiful Loire Valley, where a wealthy and powerful newspaper-owning family is involved in a number of sexual and political intrigues. It is easy to see how each attempts to enter *Dallas/Dynasty* territory. They have both met with some success.

Sales of both series have been good in Europe (not surprisingly in the case of the

*The* Coronation Street *set, built behind Granada Television's studio center in Manchester, England.*

French program, as at least five countries were financially involved in its production). Both programs have been sold to British TV, and *Schwarzwaldklinik* has been picked up in the U.S. However, they have not been as popular with international audiences as their American counterparts.

Rather more successful is Brazil's TV Globo. This company is the world's fourth largest commercial television organization after the three American networks. The soap operas they produce are by far the most popular programs on Brazilian television, and, as a result of that success, Globo decided to market them internationally. They have sold well within Latin America, despite the fact that Brazil is the only Portuguese-speaking country in the area, and in Portugal and Spain. More recently, the programs have been successful on American Spanish language stations and in the rest of Europe — particularly Italy and Britain.

TV Globo's productions are interesting because they are strikingly original. *Malu Muher*, for example, gives an unusual feminist view of women's role in soap operas; *Isaura, the Slave Girl* deals directly with questions of race and racial differences; and *Tenda Dos Milagres* (Tent of Miracles) is an adaptation of a famous novel by one of Brazil's greatest authors, Jorge Amado.

**Above** *Chantal Nobel as Florence Berg in French television's answer to* Dallas — Chateauvallon.

Lucella Santos as Escrava Isaura, The Slave Girl — *the Brazilian soap opera that deals with racial problems.*

33

# 5 Light Entertainment

Light entertainment is the third major area of production for most television companies. Thames Television, the largest of the British commercial television companies, gives its biggest budget to the light entertainment department. In 1985, the budget was $1,750,000 more than that of its nearest rival, the drama department. Drama is still the most expensive area of television production hour for hour, but the light entertainment department produced more than twice as many program hours as the drama department.

Three types of program make up the area of light entertainment: variety shows, quiz shows, and situation comedies. The first two types are usually performed in front of a "live" audience. In the case of most "sit-coms," the laughter (known as "canned" laughter) is added later, but some people argue that a light entertainment program loses a certain spontaneity unless it is filmed with a live audience.

*The live talk show, conducted in front of a studio audience, is very popular. Terry Wogan interviews Jonathan Miller on BBC's early evening show, Wogan.*

"Scuse I, Sir Les Paterson's the name!" Barry Humphries playing his comic role of Australia's Cultural Ambassador.

Barry Humphries as another of his world famous characters — Dame Edna Everage, "housewife and megastar."

## ● VARIETY SHOWS

Variety shows cover a whole range of programs, from large-scale spectaculars featuring international singing and dancing stars; comedy shows, which mix musical numbers with comedy sketches and dancers; magic shows; and zany and anarchic programs such as Milton Berle's *Texaco Star Theatre* and the British import, *Monty Python's Flying Circus*. Also included in this broad category are rock music programs such as *Top of the Pops*, and *The Tube*; circuses, ice shows and award ceremonies, such as the Academy Awards; shows like *Johnny Carson, Phil Donahue*, and *The Joan Rivers Show*; and finally that most undefinable of all shows, the biographical *This is Your Life*.

Light entertainment owes much to the old music hall and vaudeville traditions of the 1800s. The standard mixture of troupes of dancers, singers, stand-up comics, comedy sketches, and "star turns" in front of a live audience is similar to the old variety acts in theaters. For many performers, such shows are important because, since the disappearance of variety theaters, they offer a chance to work with an audience. Many comedians and talk show hosts need an audience to establish a rapport on which to build jokes. Mel Brooks and Johnny Carson would be lost without a live audience to respond to their jokes.

**Above** The Price is Right, *British-style, stars Leslie Crowther as host and differs from its U.S. counterpart in the size of the much less expensive prizes that are offered.*

**.Below** *Monte Hall, host of the game show,* Let's Make a Deal.

## ● QUIZ SHOWS

Quiz shows have always been popular television fare. Since they were introduced the prizes have become more desirable, and by the 1950s, thousands of dollars were won each month. In 1959, evidence of cheating was uncovered, and a major scandal erupted. Several shows were proven to have been rigged, and most of the shows were dropped. They have become popular again and the format has been widely copied, especially in Britain, where the main difference lies in the size of the prizes.

Game shows in the United States are broadcast throughout the morning, one after another. In Britain, they are more often scheduled at prime viewing times. They have great appeal to producers: audiences are large, and they are relatively cheap to make.

There are many kinds of quiz shows, which are generally divided into two categories — game shows, where contestants perform for fun, and "competition and reward" shows. The former includes television "parlor games," often featuring celebrities, such as *Celebrity Squares, Call My Bluff, Face the Music*, and *Child's Play*; the latter covers a range from the particularly British *Mastermind*, where the prize is simply the honor of being given the title "Mastermind" for a year to *The Price is Right*, where all you need to be able to do is to guess the value of consumer goods.

In Britain, the top prize on such shows is limited to a specific sum per week averaged out over a month. In the U.S. the sky is seemingly the limit, although the record is $264,000 in 1958.

However, the real winners would seem to be the inventors of such games — Chuck Barris reputedly earns $60 million a year simply for having devised the formula of *Blind Date*!

*Magnus Magnusson, the Question Master in the academic setting of* Mastermind, *a popular British show in which the only prize offered is the honor and prestige of being Britain's "Mastermind" for a year.*

# ● SITUATION COMEDIES

Situation comedies — or "sit-coms" as they are commonly called — seem to belong more to drama, although they are considered light entertainment. As already mentioned, they are often performed in front of a live audience and, like quiz shows, they have a format which is often sold to another country. Comedy means different things in different countries, and different cultures laugh at different situations. So it is not completely surprising that, while *Fawlty Towers* and *Yes, Minister* were sold to PBS in their original British versions, most British sit-coms are sold to the U.S. as an idea, or format. Original British sit-coms, such as *Steptoe and Son, Till Death Us Do Part*, and *Porridge*, have been re-made and re-titled in the U.S. as *Sanford and Son, All In The Family*, and *On The Rocks* respectively.

"Family" sit-coms, from *I Love Lucy* to *The Cosby Show*, have been perennial favourites with American audiences; and many of the best, including many vintage series, such as *Bewitched* and *The Munsters*, are shown regularly on screens in many other parts of the world.

**Above** *American TV buys a British format: Carroll O'Connor as the bigoted and patriotic Archie Bunker in* All In The Family, *which is based on* Till Death Us Do Part.

**Below** *Warren Mitchell as the bigoted and patriotic Alf Garnett in BBC television's sit-com* Till Death Us Do Part.

**Right** *John Cleese as the manic Basil Fawlty standing outside his hotel* Fawlty Towers. *This popular British series has a cult following.*

# 6 The New Delivery Systems

*One of the control rooms at the British headquarters of Sky Channel, a station that currently transmits programs to 14 countries.*

Cable, satellite, and video are often referred to as "the new technologies" or the "new delivery systems" of television. They have forced a major re-think of the organization of broadcasting right across the world. What are the debates about, and why are governments so concerned about these new systems?

## ● CABLE

Strictly speaking, cable is not a new technology. Cable was first introduced into the U.S. and in Britain in the 1930s for radio and the 1950s for television. Its original purpose was to provide a service for areas that experienced poor reception from geographical features such as hills or in places with many tall buildings. What is new about recent cable developments is the invention of the "fiber optic" cable.

By using laser technology, fiber optic cable can carry dozens and potentially hundreds of channels through a very thin cable. The advantage of this cable is that it can carry far more than television signals — it is possible to carry a far greater range of communication services than a telephone system. The disadvantages are that the cable is very expensive to make and to install.

Cable has been extensively installed in Belgium and Holland (81 percent and 74 percent of homes are cabled respectively), where it is extremely useful because of the multiple languages spoken in those countries. Less than 6 percent of homes in Britain are cabled; the British seem wary of installing cable, since there have been some spectacular failures involving cable television companies in the U.S.

North America is extensively cabled (nearly 40 million homes are linked up), because there

seemed to be a demand for it. In addition to overcoming interference in areas with poor reception, cable brought the promise of expanding the range of programs that would be available. The promise of, for example, movies without advertising breaks, such as the Home Box Office offers, is very attractive. Thus, people like Ted Turner with his 24-hour cable news service CNN, feel that cable offers a great expansion of the services television can provide. Cable, however, makes sense only when operated together with satellite services.

## ● SATELLITE

Communication satellites have also been used for over 20 years, and currently there are approximately 50 in operation. Originally designed for telephone and telegraph systems, they are increasingly used for transmitting television news signals from country to country.

However, the really important development in satellite technology is a system called DBS (Direct Broadcasting Satellites), which are

**Right** *Large dish aerials send TV signals up to a satellite, which then passes them on to a dish in the receiving country for transmission.*

40

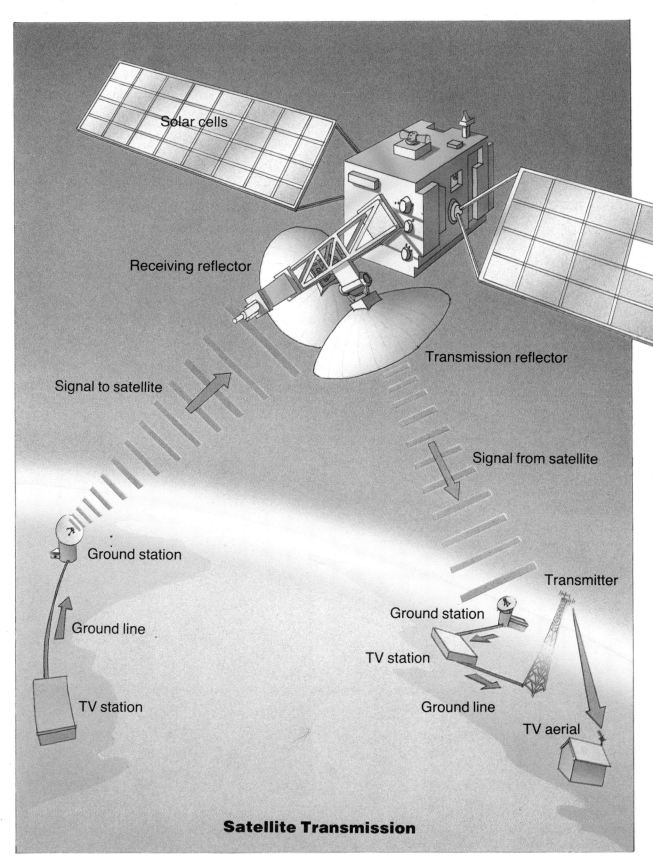

Solar cells

Receiving reflector

Transmission reflector

Signal to satellite

Signal from satellite

Ground station

Transmitter

Ground line

Ground station

TV station

TV station

Ground line

TV aerial

**Satellite Transmission**

*Broadcasts of events such as a royal wedding are received and transmitted for internal and international viewing from the British Telecom Tower in London.*

communication satellites so powerful that their signals can be picked up on a small receiving dish less than half a yard in diameter. This means that they will be small and cheap enough for individual houses to buy or rent and they will receive television programs directly from the satellite without having to be fed through a cable system.

There should already be a number in operation, but in fact, only Japan has one, which started broadcasting in 1984. The reason for the delay has been the successive failures of the two main rocket launch systems — the American Shuttle program and the French Ariane project. Nevertheless, it is clear that DBS will come and that it will make a huge difference to broadcasting, particularly in countries the size of the United States, U.S.S.R., India, Australia, China, and Brazil.

However, many people — and many governments — are worried about how the future will develop. Because the cost and technology involved is so great, it is clear that the rich and powerful will be in control of a communication system that will transmit not just to whole countries, but to entire continents. Developing countries, such as those in Latin America or Africa, already feel that they are bombarded with the media products of the rich

industrialized nations. From their viewpoint, the growth of satellite broadcasting will simply make it easier for companies like Lorimar (who produce and distribute *Dallas*) to further increase their influence and wealth.

At the same time, there is a growing concern that it is not just a matter of certain companies increasing their power, but, more strikingly, that a few individuals — media magnates — are beginning to dominate the world's media. The two most famous are the Australian-turned-American press magnate, Rupert Murdoch, and the Italian property developer, Silvio Berlusconi.

## ● MURDOCH AND BERLUSCONI

Rupert Murdoch owns more than 100 newspapers worldwide, including *The Times* and the *Sun* in Britain and the *New York Post* and the *Chicago Sun-Times* in the U.S. He also owns the the two largest commercial television stations in Australia; Twentieth Century Fox and six of the top ten independent American television stations, with which he is attempting to build a fourth American network; and Sky Channel in Britain, which is a satellite station that currently transmits 116 hours of television a week to five million homes in 14 countries!

*The Australian press baron Rupert Murdoch, who owns newspapers, television companies, and film studios in three continents.*

*Italian property developer Silvio Berlusconi now owns major television companies in Italy and France, as well as film studios in Spain.*

In addition to his other large business interests, Silvio Berlusconi owns three television channels in Italy, and in terms of audience size, he is the equal of the national broadcasting organization RAI; he owns a share in France's fifth television channel and film studios in Spain, which enables him to sell programs to Latin America. He has also been heavily involved in the French satellite broadcasting project.

This last point shows why western European governments treat people like Murdoch and Berlusconi so seriously. All the governments can control their own broadcasting systems, but it would seem that unless they act together through an organization such as the European Parliament or the European Economic Community, they are powerless against the wealth and strength of these media entrepreneurs. The Italian experience has shown the harmful effects of allowing commercial interests to dominate broadcasting. A mixture of cheap foreign imports and low-budget domestic production has, for many people, destroyed what was before 1976 a successful and well-run system.

While these battles and debates have been taking place over the last five years, another development has crept up behind broadcasters and almost taken them by surprise — video.

## ● VIDEO

The development of video has been the major media surprise of the 1980s. The growth rate figures were given in Chapter 1. The particular significance of the medium is that it is the only cheap electronic audiovisual way for individuals to produce and distribute television programs with total control. Obviously, the major broadcasting organizations (and individuals like Rupert Murdoch) are exploring and expanding the video distribution of their products, and the pop music industry is spending and making huge sums of money on pop videos. But the main significance of video is that it is the one media that the individual can actually *control.*

This control takes various forms. First of all, people can now choose what they want to watch, when they want to watch it, and with whom they wish to watch it. It can be a program or a film recorded from a television set, a film rented from a store or library, a tape borrowed from a friend, or it can be a tape shot on a video camera. Film distributors and exhibitors, broadcasters, and governments can no longer contol what is available for screening and at what times. This has led to a worry in organizations such as the National Viewers' and Listeners' Association in Britain that children might be able to view unsuitable material that they would not otherwise be able to see.

More significant has been the new opportunities offered by video. The medium has given rise to a whole new range of media practices around the world — for the first time, people and groups who have never had access to television before are beginning to make their own programs and to present their own ideas and beliefs.

Britain has seen the growth of small-scale and community video groups across the country, making and distributing programs about matters that concern them. Aboriginal groups in Australia are beginning to use video to record and communicate important issues and events in their lives, and the same things are happening in North America, Latin America, Africa, the Arab States, India, and Eastern Europe.

Video is a very difficult media for a government to control. Three recent British examples will demonstrate the point. In 1982, Granada Television in Britain made a program about the beheading of a minor Saudi Arabian princess entitled *Death of a Princess*. The Saudi government was offended by it and banned their television system from buying it. However, within 24 hours of its screening in Britain, a private tape had been flown to Saudi Arabia and was being distributed.

The news coverage of a miners' strike in Great Britain in 1984 created a controversy. Many people, including the striking miners, felt that many television news reports were biased against the miners and did not report their grievances adequately. As a result, a number of video groups combined to produce a series of video tapes called *The Miners' Tapes*, which provided an alternative view of the dispute. The tapes were distributed around the country and played at large meetings. It is estimated that more than a million people saw this quite different version of events.

In the last week of February, 1985, *Dallas* was taken off the air in Britain because of a dispute over rights between the BBC and Thames TV; at the same time, the IBA banned an ITV program about MI5 (the British Secret Service). Tapes of both programs were on sale in London within three days.

*Because of the widespread availability of video, many people are concerned that children may be able to view violent material that they would not otherwise be able to see.*

44

# Glossary

**Affiliates** Local television stations owned by a network company.

**Airwaves** The electrical energy that carries radio and TV messages spreads outward in the form of unseen waves in the atmosphere (like dropping a pebble in a pond).

**Broadcast** To transmit a program via airwaves over a wide area.

**Cable system** A system whereby TV programs are transmitted by cable (which links homes together like the telephone system) rather than over airwaves. Approximately 30 channels can be carried on a conventional cable.

**Canned laughter** Recordings of people laughing that can be dubbed into comedy programs not recorded in front of a live audience.

**Commission** When a TV program is commissioned, the broadcasting company or organization does not make the program itself, but pays a television production company to make it for them.

**Commodity** Any object or product that can be sold or exchanged.

**Deregulation** To take out of state control.

**Fiber optic** A relatively new form of cable that can carry hundreds of electronic information channels on beams of laser lights.

**Footage** Film stock (the plastic strip of film) is always measured in feet.

**Genre** A term used to describe and categorize a group of plays, novels, films, or TV programs that share common characteristics or features, such as the Western, the mystery, etc.

**High definition television** The more lines a TV screen has, the better the quality of the image. Currently the U.S., Japan, and most of Latin America run on 525 lines. Britain and the rest of the world use 625 lines. The new Sony high definition system has 1125 lines.

**Homing device** The use of an electronic signal, such as a broadcast transmission, to locate a precise geographical point.

**Magnate** A rich and powerful business person who owns and runs many large commercial companies.

**Monopoly** To be the sole supplier of a product or an area of business.

**Network** A group of radio and/or television stations, which cooperates financially to produce and then to transmit the same programs, often at the same time.

**Patent** A legal right granted to an inventor giving him or her the sole rights to develop, make, and market a product.

**Program format** The basic outline of a program which indicates who are the main characters and what their personalities are. This format is then used by all the different writers employed to write episodes of a long running series or serial.

**Propaganda** The material used to present only one side of an argument.

**Radar** A device that works out the speed and position of an object by bouncing radio waves off of it.

**Rating** The measurement that provides an indication of the size of an audience for a particular TV program.

**Receiving dish** A large dish-shaped antenna that picks up electronic signals beamed from a satellite.

**Royal charter** A legal decree made directly by a reigning monarch and not by parliament.

**Scanning** The movement of the dot of light across the lines of a television screen in order to create the television image. This dot covers all the lines every 1/25th of a second.

**Schedule** The timetable or order of programs.

**Soap opera** A term originally coined to describe a group of daytime American radio programs broadcast in the 1930s that were sponsored by washing powder companies and were aimed primarily at the female audience. More recently, the term has come to refer to long-running TV programs concerned with family affairs.

**Sponsorship** An agreement by which a company gives money to support a radio or television station in return for publicity of their products.

**Stripping** Scheduling series and serials at the same time five or six night a week. This strategy is also used occasionally for mini-series.

**Vaudeville** A form of live theater that consisted of a wide variety of song and dance acts, comedians, and magicians, which has virtually died out due to the popularity of TV light entertainment programs.

# Booklist

Bart Andrews *The TV Fun Book* (Scholastic Inc, 1981)
Griffin Beale *TV and Video* (EDC, 1983)
David Carey *Television: How It Works* (Merry Thoughts, 1968)
Glenn A. Cheney *Television in American Society* (Franklin Watts, 1983)
Mark Christensen and Cameron Stauth *The Sweeps: A Year in the Life of a Television Network* (William Morrow, 1984)
William F. Hallstead *Broadcasting Careers for You* (Lodestar Books, 1983)
Mat Irvine *TV and Video* (Franklin Watts, 1984)
William Jaspersohn *A Day in the Life of a Television News Reporter* (Little, Brown, 1981)
David Lachenbruch *Television* (Raintree Publications, 1984)
Andrew Langley *Television* (Franklin Watts, 1987)
Grace Maccarone *TV Today* (Scholastic Inc, 1983)
John R. Rider *Student Journalist and Broadcasting* (Rosen Group, 1968)
Louis Sabin *Television and Radio* (Troll Associates, 1985)
David Trainer *A Day in the Life of a TV News Reporter* (cassettes available) (Troll Associates, 1981)
Peter Wiltshire *Making Television Programmes* (Cambridge University Press, 1983)
John Yurko *Video Basics* (Prentice Hall, 1983)

# Further Information

For further information on the subjects covered in this book, please contact the following organizations:

ACADEMY OF TELEVISION ARTS AND SCIENCES, 3500 West Olive Avenue, Suite 700, Burbank CA 91505
AMERICAN FILM INSTITUTE, 2021 North Western Avenue, PO Box 27999, Los Angeles CA 90027
AMERICAN WOMEN IN RADIO AND TELEVISON, 1101 Connecticut Avenue, NW, Suite 700, Washington DC 20036
ASSOCIATION OF INDEPENDENT TELEVISION STATIONS, 1200 18th Street, NW, Suite 502, Washington DC 20036
FILM/VIDEO ARTS, 817 Broadway, New York NY 10003
INTERNATIONAL COUNCIL—National Academy of Television Arts and Sciences, 509 Madison Avenue, New York NY 10022
MUSEUM OF BROADCASTING, 1 East 53rd Street, New York NY 10022
NATIONAL ACADEMY OF TELEVISION ARTS AND SCIENCES, 110 West 57th Street, New York NY 10019
NATIONAL ASSOCIATION OF BLACK OWNED BROADCASTERS, 1730 M Street, NW, # 412, Washington DC 20036
NATIONAL ASSOCIATION OF PUBLIC TELEVISION STATIONS, 1818 N Street, NW, Suite 410, Washington DC 20036
NATIONAL CABLE TELEVISION ASSOCIATION, 1724 Massachusetts Avenue, NW, Washington DC 20036
UNESCO—Division of the Free Flow of Information and Communication Policies, United Nations Education, Science and Cultural Organization, 7 Place de Fontenoy, 75700 Paris, France

## Picture acknowledgements

The author and publishers would like to thank the following for allowing their illustrations to be reproduced in this book:
All-Sport 24, 25; Aquarius Picture Library *cover* (Jim Globus/Onyx), 4, 5 (right) (© Disney Productions), 12, 16 (NOS/TV), 17, 28 (right), 29, 30, 31 (Jim Globus/Onyx), 36 (bottom), 38 (top); BBC Enterprises 5 (left), 28 (left), 35 (both), 37, 38 (left), 39; BBC Hulton Picture Library 6 (both), 7; Central Television 36 (top); Channel Four Television 14 (top), 15, 33 (top); Granada Television 32; Sally & Richard Greenhill 44; Christine Osborne 27; PHOTRI 10; Popperfoto 20 (right); Sony Broadcast 9 (top); Telefocus 40, 42 (left); Topham Picture Library 13 (top), 14 (bottom), 18, 23, 34, 42 (right), 43; TV Globo 33 (bottom); TVS (Television South) 26; Malcolm S. Walker 8-9, 19, 41; ZEFA Picture Library 11, 20 (left), 21.

# Index